Famous LATIN HITS

— 2nd Edition —

ARRANGED BY LEE EVANS

ISBN 978-1-5400-4249-1

For all works contained herein:
Unauthorized copying, arranging, adapting, recording, Internet posting, public performance,
or other distribution of the music in this publication is an infringement of copyright.
Infringers are liable under the law.

Visit Hal Leonard Online at
www.halleonard.com

Contact us:
Hal Leonard
7777 West Bluemound Road
Milwaukee, WI 53213
Email: info@halleonard.com

In Europe, contact:
Hal Leonard Europe Limited
42 Wigmore Street
Marylebone, London, W1U 2RN
Email: info@halleonardeurope.com

In Australia, contact:
Hal Leonard Australia Pty. Ltd.
4 Lentara Court
Cheltenham, Victoria, 3192 Australia
Email: info@halleonard.com.au

ADIOS

English Words by EDDIE WOODS
Spanish Translation and Music by
ENRIC MADRIGUERA
Arranged by LEE EVANS

Verse
Steady beat (♩ = 63) (Straight 8ths)

Copyright © 1931 by Peer International Corporation
Copyright Renewed
This arrangement Copyright © 1998 by Peer International Corporation
International Copyright Secured   All Rights Reserved

AMOR
(AMOR, AMOR, AMOR)

Music by GABRIEL RUIZ
Spanish Words by RICARDO LOPEZ MENDEZ
English Words by NORMAN NEWELL
Arranged by LEE EVANS

Bright Beguine; Leggiero (♩ = 72) **(Straight 8ths)**

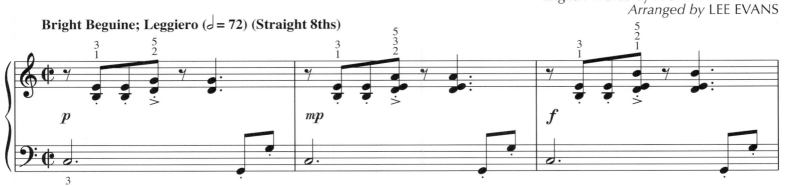

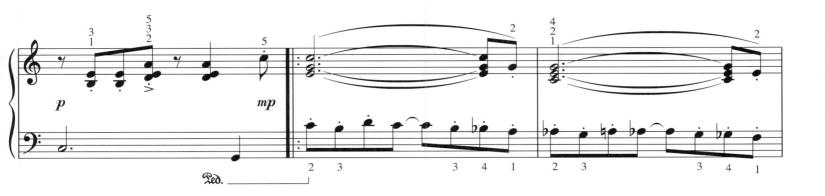

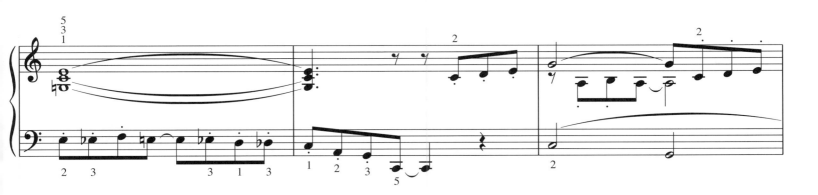

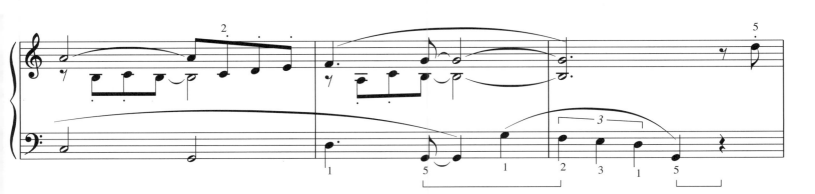

Copyright © 1941, 1943, 1963, 1964 by Promotora Hispano Americana de Musica, S.A.
Copyrights Renewed
This arrangement Copyright © 1998 by Promotora Hispano Americana de Musica, S.A.
All Rights Administered by Peer International Corporation for the World excluding Mexico and Central America
International Copyright Secured   All Rights Reserved

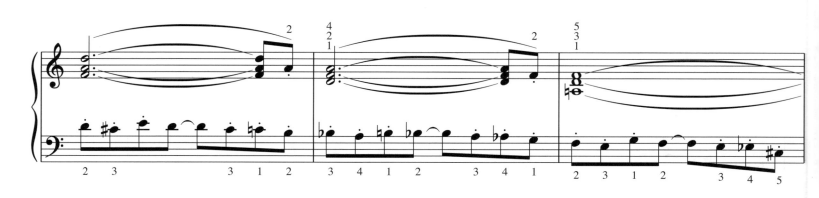

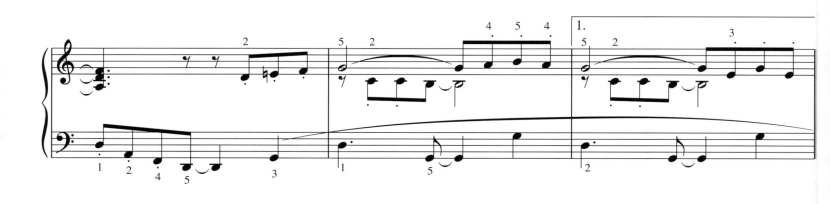

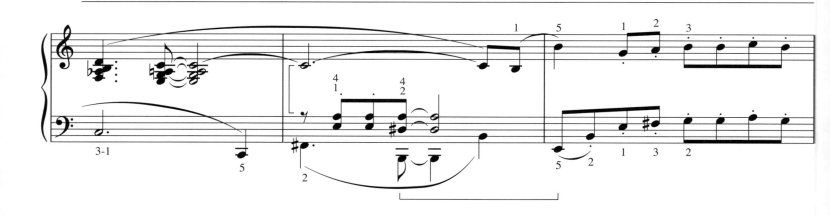

ALWAYS IN MY HEART
(SIEMPRE EN MI CORAZON)
from ALWAYS IN MY HEART

Music and Spanish Words by
ERNESTO LECUONA
English Words by KIM GANNON
Arranged by LEE EVANS

Copyright © 1942 by Southern Music Pub. Co. Inc.
Copyright Renewed
This arrangement Copyright © 1998 by Southern Music Pub. Co. Inc.
International Copyright Secured   All Rights Reserved

Chorus
Rhumba

AQUELLOS OJOS VERDES
(GREEN EYES)

Spanish Words by ADOLFO UTRERA
English Words by E. RIVERA
and E. WOODS
Arranged by LEE EVANS

Copyright © 1929, 1931 by Peer International Corporation
Copyrights Renewed
This arrangement Copyright © 1998 by Peer International Corporation
International Copyright Secured   All Rights Reserved

Chorus
Rhumba (♩ = 63) (Straight 8ths)

To Coda ⊕

BRAZIL

Original Words and Music by
ARY BARROSO
English lyrics by S. K. RUSSELL
Arranged by LEE EVANS

Bright Samba ($\mathbf{d}$ = 116)

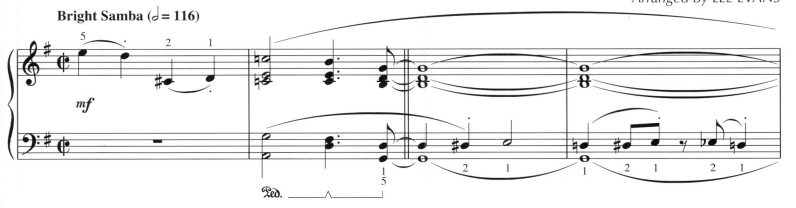

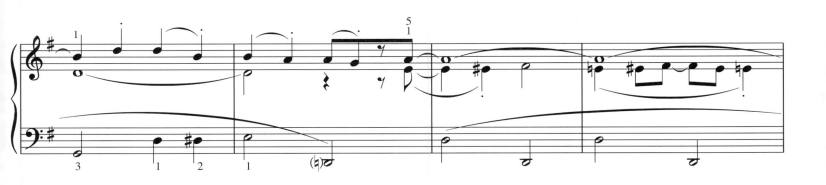

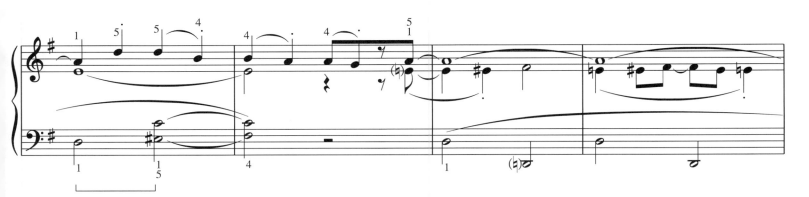

Copyright © 1941 by Irmaos Vitale S.A.
Copyright Renewed
This arrangement Copyright © 1998 by Irmaos Vitale S.A.
All Rights for the World excluding Brazil Administered by Peer International Corporation
International Copyright Secured   All Rights Reserved

To Coda ⊕

sim.

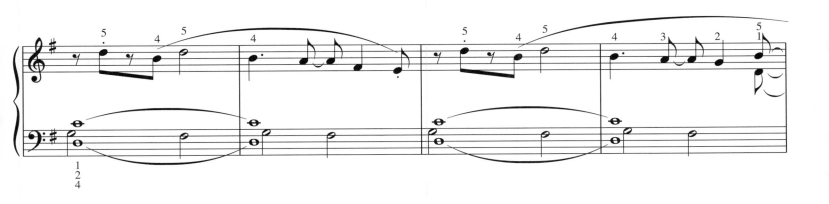

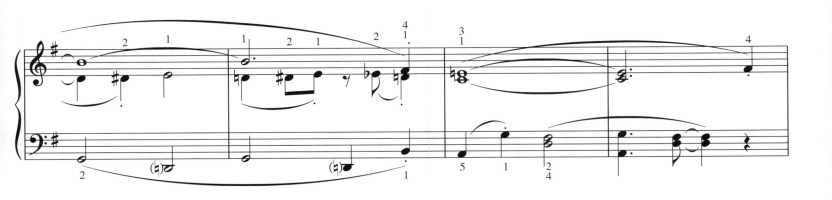

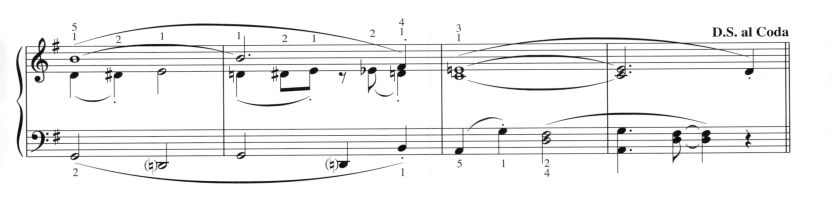

D.S. al Coda

CODA

sim.

8va -

sim.

BÉSAME MUCHO
(KISS ME MUCH)

Words and Music by
CONSUELO VELAZQUEZ
Arranged by LEE EVANS

Moderate Rhumba; Expressively (♩ = 50) (Straight 8ths)

Copyright © 1941 by Promotora Hispano Americana De Musica
Copyright Renewed
This arrangement Copyright © 1998 by Promotora Hispano Americana De Musica
All Rights Administered by Peer International Corporation
International Copyright Secured   All Rights Reserved

CODA

FRENESÍ

Words and Music by
ALBERTO DOMINGUEZ
Arranged by LEE EVANS

Rhumba (♩ = 126) (Straight 8ths)

Chorus

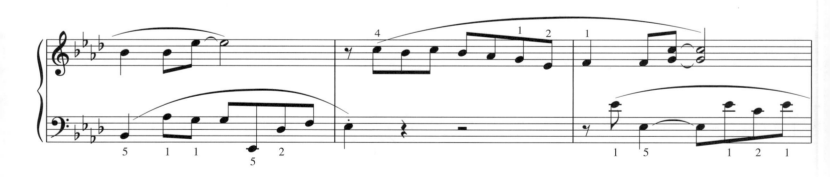

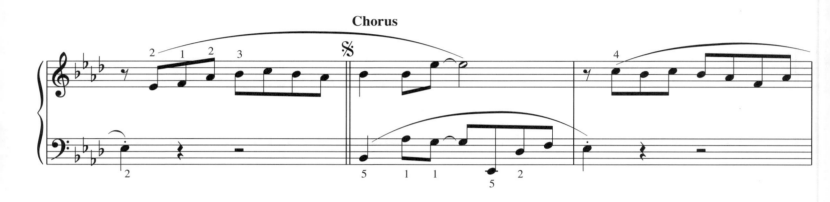

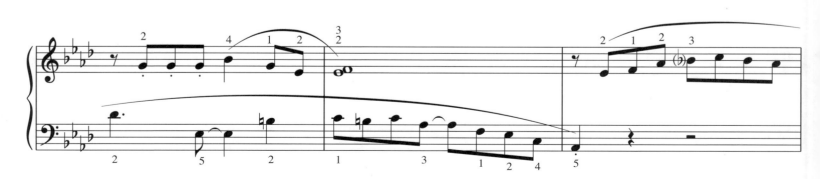

Copyright © 1939 by Peer International Corporation
Copyright Renewed
This arrangement Copyright © 1998 by Peer International Corporation
International Copyright Secured   All Rights Reserved

30

MARIA ELENA

English Words by S.K. RUSSELL
Music and Spanish Words by LORENZO BARCELATA
Arranged by LEE EVANS

Copyright © 1932 by Peer International Corporation
Copyright Renewed
This arrangement Copyright © 1998 by Peer International Corporation
International Copyright Secured   All Rights Reserved

To Coda ⊕

Verse
Slightly animated; rubato

rit.

a tempo

MAS QUE NADA

Words and Music by
JORGE BEN
Arranged by LEE EVANS

Copyright © 1963 by Peermusic do Brasil Edições Musicais Ltda.
Copyright Renewed
This arrangement Copyright © 1998 by Peermusic do Brasil Edições Musicais Ltda.
All Rights Administered by Peer International Corporation
International Copyright Secured   All Rights Reserved

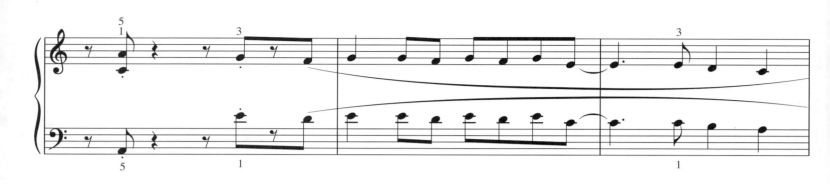

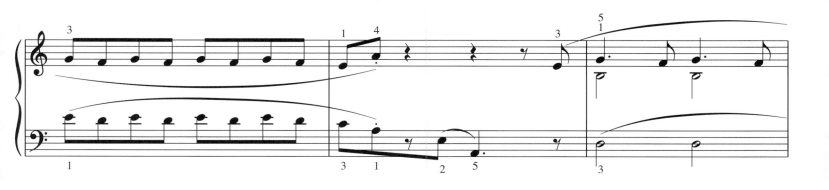

CODA

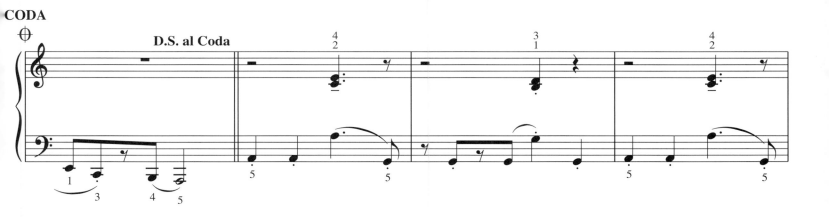

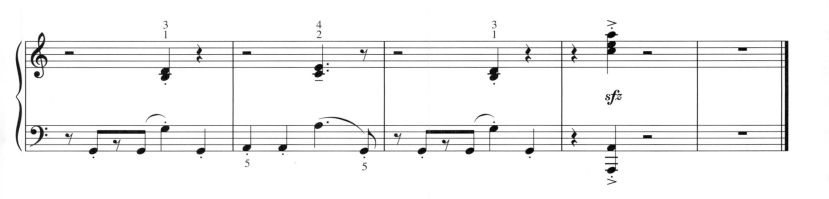

PERFIDIA

Words and Music by
ALBERTO DOMINGUEZ
Arranged by LEE EVANS

Copyright © 1939 by Peer International Corporation
Copyright Renewed
This arrangement Copyright © 1998 by Peer International Corporation
International Copyright Secured All Rights Reserved

40

THE SHADOW OF YOUR SMILE
Love Theme from THE SANDPIPER

Music by JOHNNY MANDEL
Words by PAUL FRANCIS WEBSTER
Arranged by LEE EVANS

© 1965 METRO-GOLDWYN-MAYER, INC.
Copyright Renewed by EMI MILLER CATALOG INC. and MARISSA MUSIC
This arrangement © 2018 METRO-GOLDWYN-MAYER, INC.
All Rights for EMI MILLER CATALOG INC. Controlled and Administered by EMI MILLER CATALOG INC. (Publishing) and ALFRED MUSIC (Print)
All Rights for MARISSA MUSIC Controlled and Administered by ALMO MUSIC CORP.
All Rights Reserved   Used by Permission

Chorus
Slowly

D.S. al Coda

CODA

8vb - ⌐

SWAY
(QUIEN SERA)

English Words by NORMAN GIMBEL
Spanish Words and Music by PABLO BELTRAN RUIZ
and LUIS DEMETRIO TRACONIS MOLINA
Arranged by LEE EVANS

Copyright © 1954 by Editorial Mexicana De Musica Internacional, S.A. and Words West LLC (P.O. Box 15187, Beverly Hills, CA 90209, USA)
Copyright Renewed
This arrangement Copyright © 1998 by Editorial Mexicana De Musica Internacional, S.A. and Words West LLC
All Rights for Editorial Mexicana De Musica Internacional, S.A. Administered by Peer International Corporation
International Copyright Secured   All Rights Reserved

THE THREE CABALLEROS
(AY JALISCO NO TE RAJES)
from THE THREE CABALLEROS

Music by MANUEL ESPERON
English Words by RAY GILBERT
Spanish Words by ERNESTO M. CORTAZAR
Arranged by LEE EVANS

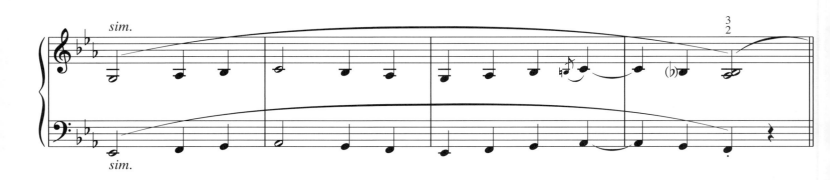

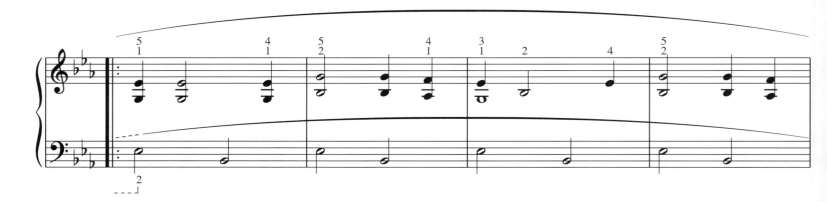

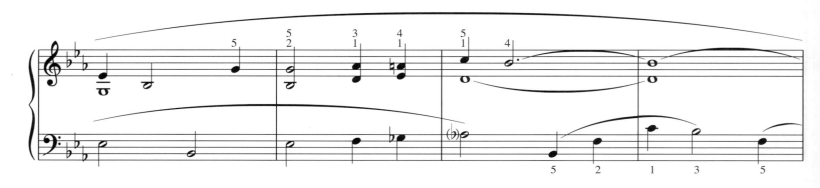

Copyright © 1944 by Peer International Corporation
Copyright Renewed
This arrangement Copyright © 1998 by Peer International Corporation
International Copyright Secured   All Rights Reserved

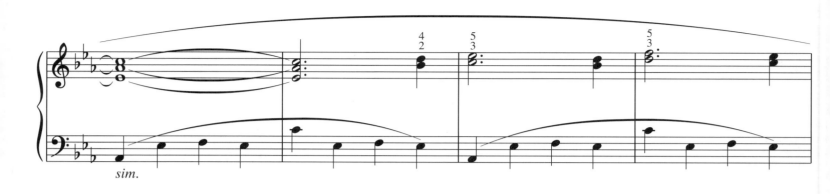

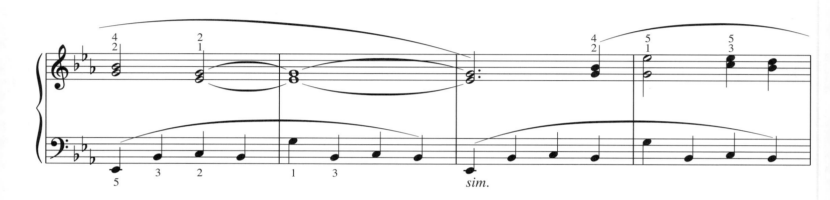

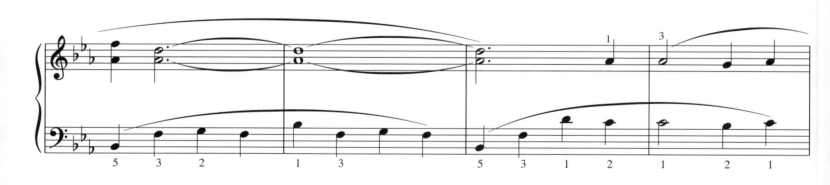

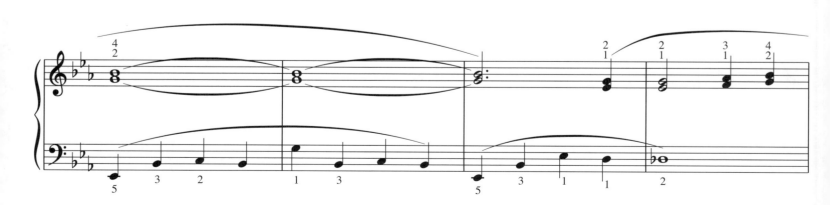

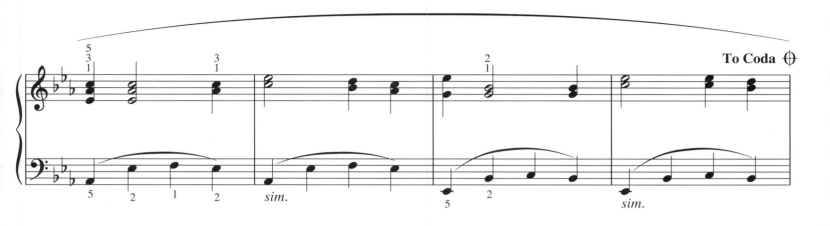

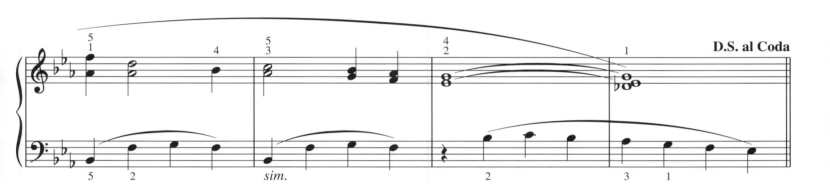

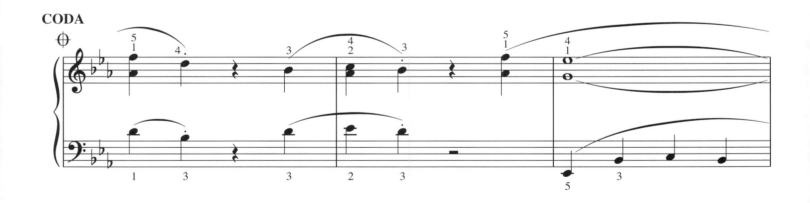

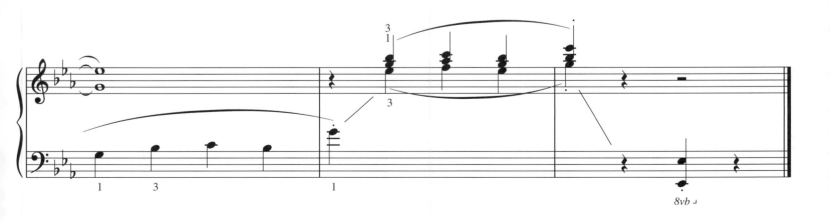

To Coda

D.S. al Coda

CODA

sim.

8vb

TICO TICO
(TICO NO FUBA)

Words and Music by ZEQUINHA ABREU,
ALOYSIO OLIVEIRA and ERVIN DRAKE
Arranged by LEE EVANS

Bright Samba; leggiero ($\circ$ = 132) (Straight 8ths)

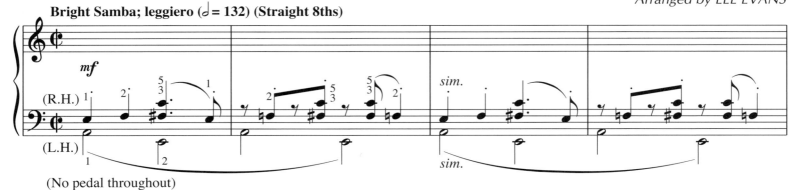

(No pedal throughout)

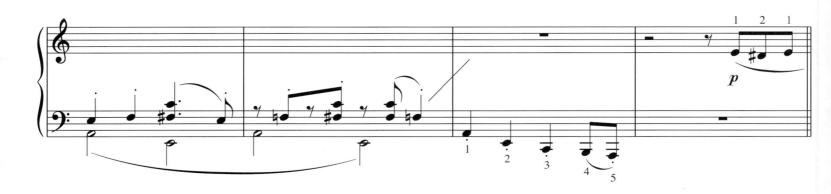

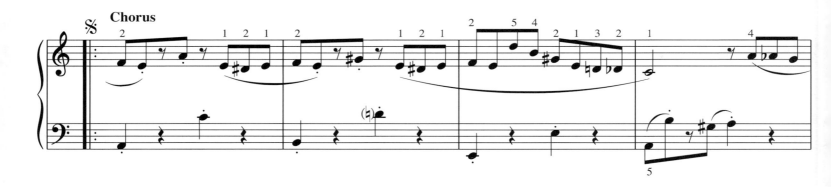

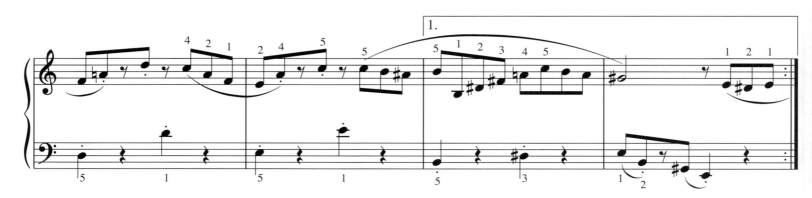

Copyright © 1943 by Irmaos Vitale S.A.
Copyright Renewed
This arrangement Copyright © 1998 by Irmaos Vitale S.A.
All Rights Administered by Peer International Corporation
International Copyright Secured   All Rights Reserved

Interlude

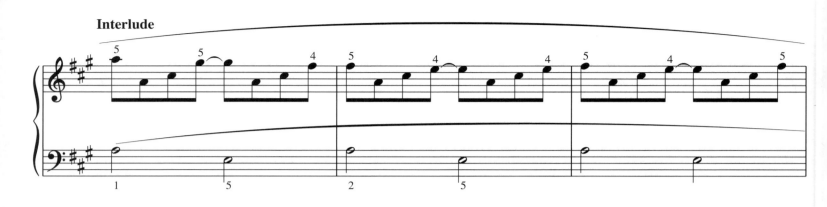

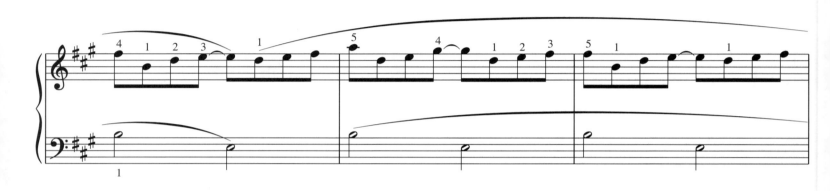

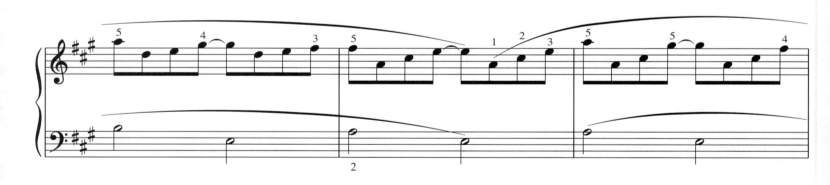

Return to Chorus
(Play full chorus again
with repeat and D.S.)

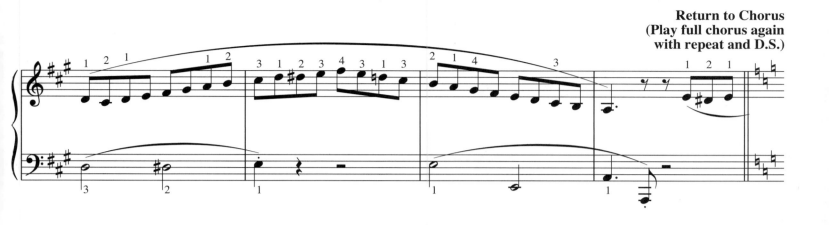

CODA

(2nd Chorus only)

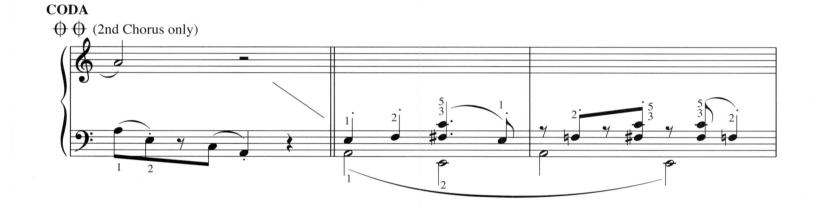

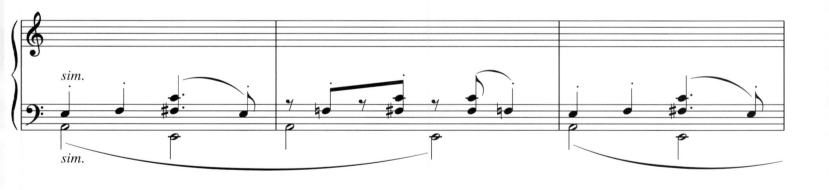

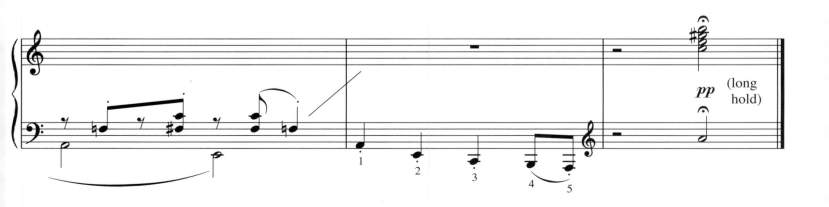

A TIME FOR LOVE
from AN AMERICAN DREAM

Music by JOHNNY MANDEL
Words by PAUL FRANCIS WEBSTER
Arranged by LEE EVANS

© 1966 (Renewed) WB MUSIC CORP.
This arrangement © 2018 (Renewed) WB MUSIC CORP.
All Rights Reserved   Used by Permission

To Coda

TRES PALABRAS
(WITHOUT YOU)

Original Words and Music by
OSVALDO FARRÉS
English Words by RAY GILBERT
Arranged by LEE EVANS

Moderate Rhumba (♩ = 72) (Straight 8ths)

Copyright © 1942 by Peer International Corporation
Copyright Renewed
This arrangement Copyright © 1998 by Peer International Corporation
International Copyright Secured   All Rights Reserved

YOU BELONG TO MY HEART
(SOLAMENTE UNA VEZ)

Words and Music by
AGUSTIN LARA
Arranged by LEE EVANS

Moderate Rhumba (♩ = 120) (Straight 8ths)

Copyright © 1941 by Promotora Hispano Americana De Musica, S.A.
Copyright Renewed
This arrangement Copyright © 1998 by Promotora Hispano Americana De Musica, S.A.
All Rights Administered by Peer International Corporation
International Copyright Secured   All Rights Reserved

KEYBOARD STYLE SERIES

THE COMPLETE GUIDE!

These book/audio packs provide focused lessons that contain valuable how-to insight, essential playing tips, and beneficial information for all players. From comping to soloing, comprehensive treatment is given to each subject. The companion audio features many of the examples in the book performed either solo or with a full band.

BEBOP JAZZ PIANO

by John Valerio

This book provides detailed information for bebop and jazz keyboardists on: chords and voicings, harmony and chord progressions, scales and tonality, common melodic figures and patterns, comping, characteristic tunes, the styles of Bud Powell and Thelonious Monk, and more.

00290535 Book/CD Pack.......................$18.99

BEGINNING ROCK KEYBOARD

by Mark Harrison

This comprehensive book/CD package will teach you the basic skills needed to play beginning rock keyboard. From comping to soloing, you'll learn the theory, the tools, and the techniques used by the pros. The accompanying CD demonstrates most of the music examples in the book.

00311922 Book/CD Pack.......................$14.99

BLUES PIANO

by Mark Harrison

With this book/audio pack, you'll learn the theory, the tools, and even the tricks that the pros use to play the blues. Covers: scales and chords; left-hand patterns; walking bass; endings and turnarounds; right-hand techniques; how to solo with blues scales; crossover licks; and more.

00311007 Book/Online Audio $19.99

BOOGIE-WOOGIE PIANO

by Todd Lowry

From learning the basic chord progressions to inventing your own melodic riffs, you'll learn the theory, tools and techniques used by the genre's best practicioners.

00117067 Book/Online Audio $17.99

BRAZILIAN PIANO

by Robert Willey and Alfredo Cardim

Brazilian Piano teaches elements of some of the most appealing Brazilian musical styles: choro, samba, and bossa nova. It starts with rhythmic training to develop the fundamental groove of Brazilian music.

00311469 Book/Online Audio $19.99

CONTEMPORARY JAZZ PIANO

by Mark Harrison

From comping to soloing, you'll learn the theory, the tools, and the techniques used by the pros. The full band tracks on the audio feature the rhythm section on the left channel and the piano on the right channel, so that you can play along with the band.

00311848 Book/Online Audio $18.99

COUNTRY PIANO

by Mark Harrison

Learn the theory, the tools, and the tricks used by the pros to get that authentic country sound. This book/audio pack covers: scales and chords, walkup and walkdown patterns, comping in traditional and modern country, Nashville "fretted piano" techniques and more.

00311052 Book/Online Audio $19.99

GOSPEL PIANO

by Kurt Cowling

Discover the tools you need to play in a variety of authentic gospel styles, through a study of rhythmic devices, grooves, melodic and harmonic techniques, and formal design. The accompanying audio features over 90 tracks, including piano examples as well as the full gospel band.

00311327 Book/Online Adio $17.99

INTRO TO JAZZ PIANO

by Mark Harrison

From comping to soloing, you'll learn the theory, the tools, and the techniques used by the pros. The accompanying audio demonstrates most of the music examples in the book. The full band tracks feature the rhythm section on the left channel and the piano on the right channel, so that you can play along with the band.

00312088 Book/Online Audio $17.99

JAZZ-BLUES PIANO

by Mark Harrison

This comprehensive book will teach you the basic skills needed to play jazz-blues piano. Topics covered include: scales and chords • harmony and voicings • progressions and comping • melodies and soloing • characteristic stylings.

00311243 Book/Online Audio $17.99

JAZZ-ROCK KEYBOARD

by T. Lavitz

Learn what goes into mixing the power and drive of rock music with the artistic elements of jazz improvisation in this comprehensive book and CD package. This instructional tool delves into scales and modes, and how they can be used with various chord progressions to develop the best in soloing chops.

00290536 Book/CD Pack.......................$17.95

LATIN JAZZ PIANO

by John Valerio

This book is divided into three sections. The first covers Afro-Cuban (Afro-Caribbean) jazz, the second section deals with Brazilian influenced jazz – Bossa Nova and Samba, and the third contains lead sheets of the tunes and instructions for the play-along audio.

00311345 Book/Online Audio $17.99

MODERN POP KEYBOARD

by Mark Harrison

From chordal comping to arpeggios and ostinatos, from grand piano to synth pads, you'll learn the theory, the tools, and the techniques used by the pros. The online audio demonstrates most of the music examples in the book.

00146596 Book/Online Audio $17.99

NEW AGE PIANO

by Todd Lowry

From melodic development to chord progressions to left-hand accompaniment patterns, you'll learn the theory, the tools and the techniques used by the pros. The accompanying 96-track CD demonstrates most of the music examples in the book.

00117322 Book/CD Pack.......................$16.99

POST-BOP JAZZ PIANO

by John Valerio

This book/audio pack will teach you the basic skills needed to play post-bop jazz piano. Learn the theory, the tools, and the tricks used by the pros to play in the style of Bill Evans, Thelonious Monk, Herbie Hancock, McCoy Tyner, Chick Corea and others. Topics covered include: chord voicings, scales and tonality, modality, and more.

00311005 Book/Online Audio $17.99

PROGRESSIVE ROCK KEYBOARD

by Dan Maske

You'll learn how soloing techniques, form, rhythmic and metrical devices, harmony, and counterpoint all come together to make this style of rock the unique and exciting genre it is.

00311307 Book/Online Audio $19.99

R&B KEYBOARD

by Mark Harrison

From soul to funk to disco to pop, you'll learn the theory, the tools, and the tricks used by the pros with this book/audio pack. Topics covered include: scales and chords, harmony and voicings, progressions and comping, rhythmic concepts, characteristic stylings, the development of R&B, and more! Includes seven songs.

00310881 Book/Online Audio $19.99

ROCK KEYBOARD

by Scott Miller

Learn to comp or solo in any of your favorite rock styles. Listen to the audio to hear your parts fit in with the total groove of the band. Includes 99 tracks! Covers: classic rock, pop/rock, blues rock, Southern rock, hard rock, progressive rock, alternative rock and heavy metal.

00310823 Book/Online Audio $17.99

ROCK 'N' ROLL PIANO

by Andy Vinter

Take your place alongside Fats Domino, Jerry Lee Lewis, Little Richard, and other legendary players of the '50s and '60s! This book/audio pack covers: left-hand patterns; basic rock 'n' roll progressions; right-hand techniques; straight eighths vs. swing eighths; glisses, crushed notes, rolls, note clusters and more. Includes six complete tunes.

00310912 Book/Online Audio $18.99

SALSA PIANO

by Hector Martignon

From traditional Cuban music to the more modern Puerto Rican and New York styles, you'll learn the all-important rhythmic patterns of salsa and how to apply them to the piano. The book provides historical, geographical and cultural background info, and the 50+-tracks includes piano examples and a full salsa band percussion section.

00311049 Book/Online Audio $19.99

SMOOTH JAZZ PIANO

by Mark Harrison

Learn the skills you need to play smooth jazz piano – the theory, the tools, and the tricks used by the pros. Topics covered include: scales and chords; harmony and voicings; progressions and comping; rhythmic concepts; melodies and soloing; characteristic stylings; discussions on jazz evolution.

00311095 Book/Online Audio $19.99

STRIDE & SWING PIANO

by John Valerio

Learn the styles of the stride and swing piano masters, such as Scott Joplin, Jimmy Yancey, Pete Johnson, Jelly Roll Morton, James P. Johnson, Fats Waller, Teddy Wilson, and Art Tatum. This book/audio pack covers classic ragtime, early blues and boogie woogie, New Orleans jazz and more. Includes 14 songs.

00310882 Book/Online Audio $19.99

WORSHIP PIANO

by Bob Kauflin

From chord inversions to color tones, from rhythmic patterns to the Nashville Numbering System, you'll learn the tools and techniques needed to play piano or keyboard in a modern worship setting.

00311425 Book/Online Audio $17.99

HAL•LEONARD®

Prices, contents, and availability
subject to change without notice.

www.halleonard.com

Creative PIANO SOLO

Looking to add some variety to your playing? Enjoy these beautifully distinctive arrangements for piano solo! These popular tunes get new and unique treatments for a fun and fresh presentation. Explore new styles and enjoy these favorites with a bit of a twist! Each collection includes 20 songs for the intermediate to advanced player.

CHRISTMAS CAROLS

Away in a Manger • Deck the Hall • The First Noel • God Rest Ye Merry, Gentlemen • Hark! the Herald Angels Sing • It Came upon the Midnight Clear • Jingle Bells • Joy to the World • O Holy Night • Silent Night • Up on the Housetop • We Three Kings of Orient Are • What Child Is This? • and more.

00147214 Piano Solo $14.99

CHRISTMAS COLLECTION

Blue Christmas • The Christmas Song (Chestnuts Roasting on an Open Fire) • Frosty the Snow Man • Here Comes Santa Claus (Right down Santa Claus Lane) • Let It Snow! Let It Snow! Let It Snow! • Silver Bells • Sleigh Ride • White Christmas • Winter Wonderland • and more.

00172042 Piano Solo $14.99

CLASSIC ROCK

Another One Bites the Dust • Aqualung • Beast of Burden • Born to Be Wild • Carry on Wayward Son • Layla • Owner of a Lonely Heart • Roxanne • Smoke on the Water • Sweet Emotion • Takin' It to the Streets • 25 or 6 to 4 • Welcome to the Jungle • and more!

00138517 Piano Solo $14.99

JAZZ POP SONGS

Don't Know Why • I Just Called to Say I Love You • I Put a Spell on You • Just the Way You Are • Killing Me Softly with His Song • Mack the Knife • Michelle • Smooth Operator • Sunny • Take Five • What a Wonderful World • and more.

00195426 Piano Solo $14.99

POP BALLADS

Against All Odds (Take a Look at Me Now) • Bridge over Troubled Water • Fields of Gold • Hello • I Want to Know What Love Is • Imagine • In Your Eyes • Let It Be • She's Got a Way • Total Eclipse of the Heart • You Are So Beautiful • Your Song • and more.

00195425 Piano Solo $14.99

POP HITS

Billie Jean • Fields of Gold • Get Lucky • Happy • Ho Hey • I'm Yours • Just the Way You Are • Let It Go • Poker Face • Radioactive • Roar • Rolling in the Deep • Royals • Smells like Teen Spirit • Viva la Vida • Wonderwall • and more.

00138156 Piano Solo $14.99

Prices, contents, and availability subject to change without notice.

HAL•LEONARD®

www.halleonard.com

PLAY PIANO LIKE A PRO!

AMAZING PHRASING – KEYBOARD
50 Ways to Improve Your Improvisational Skills
by Debbie Denke
Amazing Phrasing is for any keyboard player interested in learning how to improvise and how to improve their creative phrasing. This method is divided into three parts: melody, harmony, and rhythm & style. The online audio contains 44 full-band demos for listening, as well as many play-along examples so you can practice improvising over various musical styles and progressions.
00842030 Book/Online Audio............................... $16.99

BEBOP LICKS FOR PIANO
A Dictionary of Melodic Ideas for Improvisation
by Les Wise
Written for the musician who is interested in acquiring a firm foundation for playing jazz, this unique book/audio pack presents over 800 licks. By building up a vocabulary of these licks, players can connect them together in endless possibilities to form larger phrases and complete solos. The book includes piano notation, and the online audio contains helpful note-for-note demos of every lick.
00311854 Book/Online Audio............................... $16.99

BOOGIE WOOGIE FOR BEGINNERS
by Frank Paparelli
A short easy method for learning to play boogie woogie, designed for the beginner and average pianist. Includes: exercises for developing left-hand bass • 25 popular boogie woogie bass patterns • arrangements of "Down the Road a Piece" and "Answer to the Prayer" by well-known pianists • a glossary of musical terms for dynamics, tempo and style.
00120517 .... $10.99

INTROS, ENDINGS & TURNAROUNDS FOR KEYBOARD
Essential Phrases for Swing, Latin, Jazz Waltz, and Blues Styles
by John Valerio
Learn the intros, endings and turnarounds that all of the pros know and use! This new keyboard instruction book by John Valerio covers swing styles, ballads, Latin tunes, jazz waltzes, blues, major and minor keys, vamps and pedal tones, and more.
00290525 .... $12.99

JAZZ PIANO TECHNIQUE
Exercises, Etudes & Ideas for Building Chops
by John Valerio
This one-of-a-kind book applies traditional technique exercises to specific jazz piano needs. Topics include: scales (major, minor, chromatic, pentatonic, etc.), arpeggios (triads, seventh chords, upper structures), finger independence exercises (static position, held notes, Hanon exercises), parallel interval scales and exercises (thirds, fourths, tritones, fifths, sixths, octaves), and more! The online audio includes 45 recorded examples.
00312059 Book/Online Audio............................... $19.99

JAZZ PIANO VOICINGS
An Essential Resource for Aspiring Jazz Musicians
by Rob Mullins
The jazz idiom can often appear mysterious and difficult for musicians who were trained to play other types of music. Long-time performer and educator Rob Mullins helps players enter the jazz world by providing voicings that will help the player develop skills in the jazz genre and start sounding professional right away – without years of study! Includes a "Numeric Voicing Chart," chord indexes in all 12 keys, info about what range of the instrument you can play chords in, and a beginning approach to bass lines.
00310914 .... $19.99

OSCAR PETERSON – JAZZ EXERCISES, MINUETS, ETUDES & PIECES FOR PIANO
Legendary jazz pianist Oscar Peterson has long been devoted to the education of piano students. In this book he offers dozens of pieces designed to empower the student, whether novice or classically trained, with the technique needed to become an accomplished jazz pianist.
00311225 .... $14.99

PIANO AEROBICS
by Wayne Hawkins
Piano Aerobics is a set of exercises that introduces students to many popular styles of music, including jazz, salsa, swing, rock, blues, new age, gospel, stride, and bossa nova. In addition, there is a online audio with accompaniment tracks featuring professional musicians playing in those styles.
00311863 Book/Online Audio............................... $19.99

PIANO FITNESS
A Complete Workout
by Mark Harrison
This book will give you a thorough technical workout, while having fun at the same time! The accompanying online audio allows you to play along with a rhythm section as you practice your scales, arpeggios, and chords in all keys. Instead of avoiding technique exercises because they seem too tedious or difficult, you'll look forward to playing them. Various voicings and rhythmic settings, which are extremely useful in a variety of pop and jazz styles, are also introduced.
00311995 Book/Online Audio............................... $19.99

THE TOTAL KEYBOARD PLAYER
A Complete Guide to the Sounds, Styles & Sonic Spectrum
by Dave Adler
Do you play the keyboards in your sleep? Do you live for the feel of the keys beneath your fingers? If you answered in the affirmative, then read on, brave musical warrior! All you seek is here: the history, the tricks, the stops, the patches, the plays, the holds, the fingering, the dynamics, the exercises, the magic. Everything you always wanted to know about keyboards, all in one amazing key-centric compendium.
00311977 Book/CD Pack $19.99

HAL•LEONARD®
7777 W. BLUEMOUND RD. P.O. BOX 13819
MILWAUKEE, WISCONSIN 53213
www.halleonard.com

Prices, contents, and availability subject to change without notice.

1018
057